The Strange Museum

by the same author

A STATE OF JUSTICE (Faber and Faber)
THOMAS HARDY : THE POETRY OF PERCEPTION (Macmillan)

The Strange Museum

TOM PAULIN

FABER AND FABER
London & Boston

First published in 1980
by Faber and Faber Limited
3 Queen Square London WC1N 3AU
Printed in Great Britain by
The Bowering Press Ltd,
Plymouth and London

© Tom Paulin 1980

British Library Cataloguing in Publication Data

Paulin, Tom
  The strange museum.
  I. Title
  821'.9' 14   PR6066 .A884S/
  ISBN 0–571–11511–X

FOR MY MOTHER AND FATHER

Contents

Acknowledgements

Some of these poems have appeared in: *Encounter, Honest Ulsterman, London Magazine, New Poetry 4, New Statesman, Poetry Book Society Christmas Supplement,* 'Poetry Now' (Radio 3), *Poetry Review, Renaissance and Modern Studies, Stand, The New Review, The Times Literary Supplement;* and some have also appeared in a pamphlet, *Personal Column* (Ulsterman Publications).

Before History

Mornings when I wake too early.
There is a dead light in the room.
Rain is falling through the darkness
And the yellow lamps of the city
Are flared smudges on the wet roads.
Everyone is sleeping. I envy them.
I lie in a curtained room.
The city is nowhere then.
Somewhere, in a dank *mitteleuropa*,
I have gone to ground in a hidden street.

This is the long lulled pause
Before history happens,
When the spirit hungers for form,
Knowing that love is as distant
As the guarded capital, knowing
That the tyranny of memories
And factual establishments
Has stretched to its breaking.

Personal Column

These messages are secret, the initials
Code them, puzzling most of us. 'LY
Where are you now? I love you still. MN'.
And then, next evening, 'MN are you still there?
Loving you. LY.' Until, 'Shall I write
To old address?' MN suggests, waiting.

Each teatime, the thin signals start again.
You can almost hear the cheeping
Of separated loves, obscure adulteries
That finished in pub carparks, though they want
To make it new, to meet again, furtively,
Like spies whose thoughts touch before their bodies can.

Love, in an empty warehouse, might be like this.
To think small print, so public, can be tender.
Who'd guess that in a city where the news
Is normal, so many men and women wait
For the paper-boy, their go-between, to bring them
Lonely but hopeful, to a bed somewhere?

Song for February

In a dull and metric month,
A season of dank cardboard,
There is a cheery trill
Of schmaltz and egg whisks
Behind the double-glazing
Of a million spongy lounges.
Light verse is now the norm

And academic fellows
File limericks by the score.
In a brute and sallow light
Like the cheeks of an average
Punk, dead-headed roses waste
Over the pocked snow . . .
A fucked-up future snubs

The deadlands of the mullahs
Where young men dream of laws
As simple as the gallows.
And tonto in the dreck
Below the thermocline
An appetite for sex
Exhausts its fantasies.

Bored and parched, a torpid hack
Ghosts a tenth-rate life
Of President Sunsetsuma,
While Apollo pulls a string
Of ersatz novels from his lips.
The angel chimes go *ting-a-ling*
And the sugar hostess weeps

One year in four, but more and more.

The Civil Lovers

An after-kiss, it's kind of formal,
Like saying thank you for a supper.
Odd the thresholds we retreat from,
Uttering cries and all the normal
Decencies we've been brought up on.
After our feast of skin and fur
(Its carnal anger and its screaming),
We think such ritual blessings proper.

Many the couples who lie dreaming
In a coldly separate stillness
Of a talkative forgiveness
And a love that cannot weep.
But after knowledge comes a dull
Politeness and the wish to sleep.

Purity

Perhaps a maritime pastoral
Is the form best suited
To a northern capital
With its docks and gantries,
An oil refinery on the salt marsh.

Far from the playful celebration
Of good manners on a green field
There is always that dream
Of duck-down and eider,
The lichened island whose sour light
Lets us be ourselves.

Those luminous privacies
On a bleached coast
Are fierce and authentic,
And some of us believe in them.
They are the polities of love.

But in the brilliant distance
I see a crowded troopship
Moving down the blue lough
On a summer's morning,
Its anal colours
Almost fresh in the sun.
Those black boots are shining.
There is only a pink blur
Of identical features.

Surveillances

In the winter dusk
You see the prison camp
With its blank watchtowers;
It is as inevitable
As the movement of equipment
Or the car that carries you
Towards a violent district.

In the violet light
You watch a helicopter
Circling above the packed houses,
A long beam of light
Probing streets and waste ground.
All this might be happening
Underwater.

And if you would swop its functions
For a culture of bungalows
And light verse,
You know this is one
Of the places you belong in,
And that its public uniform
Has claimed your service.

Traces

They are so light,
Those airmail letters.
Their blueness has fallen
From an Indian sky,
The hot taut atmosphere
Above the muddled village
Your parents write from.

'With God's help,
The crops have been brought
Safely in. All here
Are well, ten *lakhs* of rupees
Our lands are worth now.
That boy's father has twenty acres.
The buffalo are fine,
Though the heat is hard to bear.'

All the fierce passions
Of family and property
Are dictated to a scribe
Who understands English,
Has a daughter to marry
And a dusty handful
Of aluminium coins.

Without Knowledge

In the dead middle of the afternoon
When nothing happens and the light is dull
The will fastens itself on every object
In the room, clamping cups to the table,
Each chair to the floor. There is no sound then,
And only anger can break its tyranny,
The gentler evenings when the lights come on.

In the Meat-Safe

There is a functional greyness
where the banal, but unusual,
has found a graceless permanence
that only the odd can admire.
Those collectors of cigarette cards
and worthless believe-it-or-not facts,
are the antiquarians of corroded
appliances who worship a dullness
as lonely as the fattest man in the world.

Solemn gaberdines, they cherish
the sweat of broken wirelesses,
goose-pimples on zinc canisters,
pre-war electric razors, sticks
of worn shaving soap, bakelite
gadgets, enemas, ration cards,
contraceptive coils that once fed
safe passions in colourless rooms
chilled by utility furniture.

Most of all they delight in
the stubble that grows on dead chins.
Recording their drab histories
in back issues of *Exchange & Mart*,
they swop this confidence—that,
in the cheap hell of starlets' accents
twittering in faded movies,
someone will sing of tinned kippers
and an ultimate boredom.

Still Century

The hard captains of industry
Held the province in a firm control.

Judges, your pious tyranny
Is baked bone-dry in the old

Bricks of a hundred linen mills,
The shadows of black tabernacles.

A crowd moves along the Shankill,
And lamps shine in the dull

Streets where a fierce religion
Prays to the names of power:

Ewart and Bryson, Craig and Carson.
On every wall, texts or a thick char.

Stacked in the corners of factory-yards,
The wicker carboys of green acid

Hold out their bitter promise of whiteness
To the bleachgreens above the city.

The orange smoke at sunset, the gruff
Accents of a thousand foremen, speak

To the chosen, saying they are the stuff
That visions, cutlery and Belleek

China are laid on. They are tied
To the shade of a bearded god,

Their dream of happiness is his smile
And his skilful way with the hardest rod.

Anonymous Biography

The third notebook proves he caught a train
to the capital that April
(according to *The Times* it rained all month,
so he could have worn one of the quilted
gaberdines that were in fashion then).

A loose sheet notes the shape of a girl's face;
a cross in the margin shows he achieved
full sexual intercourse on that visit.
Also he ate a large dinner at his club
and swopped ghost stories with a velvet bishop.

His grave is visited, and scholars nail
clues to his life in parish registers :
the usual grubby secrets and possible
scandals give most of us a dry thrill.
And yet, when we watch this entangled

spirit falling in love or leaving
on that *winterreise* to the Caucasus,
there is this quickened difference—as though
any moment he may come strolling
up the street, carrying a bottle of wine

and looking as happy as himself.

An Authorized Fear

No man is completely safe. Only money
And a snug flat can help him. His furniture.

That moral landslip, the last generation,
Is waiting to drop its anger on his back.

It waits in the sun if you look into it.
The flames slam out from where your father's burning.

Some people are useful, though. I've time for them.
Like the woman who gives me suppers and talk.

She is witty, but plain, and when I leave her
I always feel I should pay more than just thanks.

But love, like fear, is contagious. And all
My relations are guilts, bad debts I could owe.

On chill spring evenings her paleness stares at me
In the clean room, its daffodils and brasses

Near her white skin. The fire set, but not burning.
The knowledge I expect is nameless to me.

'The thing you missed is what you feared and wait for,
You can go now.' What is it that I don't know?

I look into faces, see grief in strangers,
But not the thing I fear. So I watch them there,

Spending tears and wasting their allotted time,
Mourners who stand weeping in a dead garden.

Hidden Face

Her evenings are silk, a gentleness;
but the hot afternoons when her mother
bargains in the dusty market
for those two red saris that mean
she'll be married soon,
dry away her belief
in the boy she'll belong to.

The women crouch by the fire.
The sweet bitterness of the smoke blinds them
and each chappatti burns their fingers.
The pump clanks
and draws a pure water from the tubewell—
now the men bath
like patriarchs in the wide tank.
She serves them yoghurt in brass dishes.

When lights come on in the village
and a servant pads across the courtyard
to close the gates,
she walks softly on the flat roof
and gazes into a warm darkness
that might hide a face she's never seen.

If she could only walk out to meet him,
This lover who shares her sadness.

Pot Burial

He has married again. His wife
Buys ornaments and places them
On the dark sideboard. Year by year
Her vases and small jugs crowd out
The smiles of the wife who died.

Second-Rate Republics

The dull ripe smell of gas,
A pile of envelopes fading
On the hall table—no one
In this rented atmosphere remembers
The names who once gave this address.

We might be forgotten already,
She thinks, as she climbs the stairs
To spend a long weekend with him.
The trees in these brick avenues
Are showing full and green
Against the windows of partitioned rooms.
The air is humid, and down the street
She hears the single bark
Of a car door slamming shut.

He touches her and she sees herself
Being forced back into a shabby city
Somewhere else in Europe : how clammy
It is, how the crowds press and slacken
On the pavement, shaking photographs
Of a statesman's curdled face.

Now there is only a thin sheet
Between their struggling bodies
And the stained mattress.
Now his face hardens like a photograph,
And in the distance she hears
The forced jubilance of a crowd
That is desolate and obedient.

In the Lost Province

As it comes back, brick by smoky brick,
I say to myself—strange I lived there
And walked those streets. It is the Ormeau Road
On a summer's evening, a haze of absence
Over the caked city, that slumped smell
From the blackened gasworks. Ah, those brick canyons
Where Brookeborough unsheathes a sabre,
Shouting 'No Surrender' from the back of a lorry.

And the sky is a dry purple, and men
Are talking politics in a back room.
Is it too early or too late for change?
Certainly the province is most peaceful.
Who would dream of necessity, the angers
Of Leviathan, or the years of judgement?

The Harbour in the Evening

The bereaved years, they've settled to this
Bay-windowed guest house by the harbour wall.
Each of us loved a man who died,
Then learnt how to be old and seem cheerful.
I think of being young, in the coastguard station.
Those cement cottages with the washing
Swaying in the sea wind. What can she see,
The girl I talk to? Victorian childhoods
Where little stick figures go flickering
Along the roads? Such eagerness that used to be.
A butcher's shop, a boarding house, the dead
Are smiling from the windows there.
So many names, faces, and used things.
Dry calico, the smell of cedar wood . . .
I keep them in a drowsy kind of wisdom.
I have my drawer of rings and photographs.

The waves rustle on the beach like starched silk.
And girls come walking down a staircase
Into a wide room where lamps are burning.
Love was a danger and then children.
At sunset, when I saw the white beacon
On the quay, I felt a tear starting.
But I was happy like a woman who opens a door
And hears music. It was your face I saw.
I heard your voice, its gentleness.
And I stared over the water at another coast,
An old woman in a sleep of voices.

A Partial State

Intractable and northern,
dry in the sun when it shines,
otherwise rained on, justly.

White god to desert god, 'The
lines are open, what you do
to your helots is up to

you, no concern of ours. Say
no if you like, but keep them
quiet. Never forget that

irony is the weapon
of the disarmed, that yours are
blunter instruments, dourness.'

*

The chosen, having broken
their enemies, scattered them
in backstreets and tight estates.

Patriarch and matriarch,
industry and green hills, no
balance of power. Just safety.

Stillness, without history;
until leviathan spouts,
bursting through manhole covers

in the streets, making phones ring on
bare desks. 'The minister is
playing golf, please try later.'

*

Special constables train their
machine guns on council flats;
water-cannons, fire, darkness.

The clocks are bleeding now on
public buildings. Their mottoes,
emblems of failure, tell us :

*What the wrong gods established
no army can ever save.*

Line on the Grass

Shadow in the mind,
this is its territory:
a sweep of broken ground
between two guarded towns.

A tank engine rusting
in the long grass, a man
with a fly rod wading
in the grey river.

This looks so fixed, it could
be anytime; but, scanned
in the daylight, the fields
of crops, their hawthorn hedges,

seem too visible. The men
riding black bikes stiffly
along the road are passing
a burnt-out customs post

on an asphalt apron.
They are observed passing,
passing, in a dull light:
civilians at four o'clock.

Going in the Rain

An Adam house among tall trees
Whose glaucous shadows make the lawn
A still pool; bracken on the screes
Wedged above a lichened bawn;
A rectory on a broken coast ...

Our journey notices these things
Which aid the sense of being lost
In a scoured countryside that clings
To idols someone else imagined.

Georgian architects, ironic
Deists, crossed over from the mainland
To build a culture brick by brick,
And graft their reason to a state
The rain is washing out of shape.

Without Mercy

He wakes, a traveller through the horny gates,
Safe with the luggage of himself.
With the freight of dreams, anger and stiff tissue.

To have struggled through the dark again,
Where he recognized that man, Aeneas,
Burdened with a father and all the guilts

Of ruined childhood, is to have won again
And found the state stable and enduring,
As hard and proud as the body of a man

Who has travelled to the middle years
And known them fixed and dull, a dry place
Where the weak scatter when he breathes.

And in this less-than-classic dawn he knows
That judges pray only to the law of men.
They are stretched even as the men they stretch.

The Noon of Bodies

We've hardly spoken now for days.
This dry summer, its heat and silence
Hold a blue clearness always,
And the white houses throw a glare
Of burning limewash on the street's tense
Boredom which might almost share
The banal stale atmosphere that frays
Inside the narrow room we've rented.

The light falls on an unmade bed,
Hard, oppressive, like this desert air
Which turns the grace of being naked
Into a sour shame that makes us gaze
Away, guilty lovers who prefer
To think our acts had innocence.

In the Egyptian Gardens

A white mansion among cypress trees,
You will find histories inside it.
Bronze pins and sheaves of flax,
The dry shadows of a culture.

How many bibles make a Sabbath?
How many girls have disappeared
Down musky avenues of leaves?
It's an autocracy, the past.
Somewhere costive and unchanging.

I love it, but I had to leave.
The rain is falling even now,
And hell is very like those Sunday streets
Where ministers and councillors
Climb out of graves and curse at me.

The Idea in History

A Saturday dawn, the rain
Seething in the street outside.
My furniture is dark.

First novels begin like this,
A youth waking to a world
Of objects that reflect him.

Out of a soft starfish
The first eye opened
To a pure shrill light.

When the mind grew formal,
Caught in the nets of class,
History became carpets, chairs.

Surfacing like a white fish,
A consciousness is forming.
It travels from bland minsters

To snowcem estates, ideal
Under mountains that were wet,
Bare, until the builders came.

Anastasia McLaughlin

Her father is sick. He dozes most afternoons.
The nurse makes tea then and scans *The Newsletter*.
She has little to say to his grey daughter
Whose name began a strangeness the years took over.
His trade was flax and yarns, he brought her name
With an ikon and *matrioshka*—gifts for his wife
Who died the year that Carson's statue was unveiled.

McLaughlin is dreaming of a sermon he once heard
From a righteous preacher in a wooden pulpit
Who frowned upon a sinful brotherhood and shouted
The Word of deserts and rainy places where the Just
Are stretched to do the work a hard God sent them for.
His text was taken from the land of Uz
Where men are upright and their farms are walled.

'Though we may make sand to melt in a furnace
And make a mirror of it, we are as shadows
Thrown by a weaver's shuttle : and though we hide ourselves
In desolate cities and in empty houses,
His anger will seek us out till we shall hear
The accent of the destroyer, the sly champing
Of moths busy with the linen in our chests.'

He wakes to a dull afternoon like any other—
The musty dampness of his study, the window panes
That flaw his view of the lawn and settled trees.
The logs in the grate have turned to a soft ash.
The dour gardener who cut them is smoking
In the warm greenhouse, wondering did his nephew
Break in the week before and thieve McLaughlin's silver?

Constables came to the Mill House with alsatians,
And the wet spring was filled with uniforms and statements.
When they found nothing, they suspected everyone.
Even the plain woman who served them tea.
'Father, I am the lost daughter whose name you stole.
Your visions slide across these walls : dry lavender,
Old memories of all that wronged us. I am unkind.'

He sees his son below the bruised Atlantic,
And on a summer's morning in Great Victoria Street
He talks with Thomas Ferguson outside the Iceworks.
He sees the north stretched out upon the mountains,
Its dream of fair weather rubbing a bloom on rinsed slates;
He watches the mills prosper and grow derelict,
As he starts his journey to the Finland Station.

Atlantic Changelings

The breakers, the marram dunes,
A sea snipe beating over green water,
Footprints of passing visitors
On a curved strand . . . I trace them now
Like a hunched detective scowling
In a dead resort, and learn the gossip
Of a social summer—see this walled pit
Scooped by that peculiar child
No one invited to their sandy picnic.
See where Long walked his dog last evening
And where the professor's wife met him
By the tideline. They exchanged polite words
On its drift of dry shells, though a sea potato
In the likeness of a shaved pudendum
Splintered their good manners.

Far from their different societies
The scuffed patterns of these prints
Show everyone changed into transparent
Shadows, meeting on this shore.
Their inquisitive uplifted faces
Challenge and beckon with a shy
Confidence, their soothed voices
Come floating from the class
I could belong to (like them I have left
The city to consume a wild landscape).
We will pack soon and the sly locals
Will repossess this expensive view.
In the windy now I hug my righteousness
Like a thermos flask. I cry out
For a great change in nature.

Trotsky in Finland

(an incident from his memoirs)

The pension is very quiet. It is called
Rauha, meaning 'peace' in Finnish.
The air is transparent, perfecting
The pine trees and lakes.
He finds himself admiring the stillness
Of a pure landscape. He consumes it.
A bourgeois moment. It might be somewhere Swiss,
The wooden cuckoos calling to an uneventful
Absence, their polyglot puns
Melting in Trieste or Zürich.

The last days of autumn. The Swedish writer
Adds another sonnet to his cycle.
His English mistress drifts through the garden.
An actress, she admires her face
Bloomed in the smooth lake.
At night her giggles and frills dismay
The strictness of minor art.

They leave without paying their bill.

The owner chases them to Helsingfors.
His invisible wife is lying in the room
Above—they must give her champagne
To keep her heart beating, but she dies
While her husband screams for his money.
The head-waiter sets out to find him.
Leaving a crate of gilded bottles
By the corpse upstairs.
                    The silence here.
A thick snow is falling, the house
Is a dead monument. Insanely traditional.

He is completely alone. At nightfall
The postman carries a storm in his satchel:
The St. Petersburg papers, the strike is spreading.
He asks the thin boy for his bill.
He calls for horses. Thinking,
'If this were a fiction, it would be Byron
Riding out of the Tivoli Gardens, his rank
And name set aside. Forced by more than himself.'

He crosses the frontier and speaks
To a massed force at the Institute,

Plunging from stillness into history.

A Frame, an Anniversary

That sideways glance
From the door of a firelit living-room
In a bitter province
Is an angered look
At you posed in the costume
All Indian girls must wear
On their wedding-day.

And if, once,
I lifted those crimson silks
To let our bodies prove our love,
All I believe in now
Is the fact of distance
In the winter season,
The same province.

The Strange Museum

First I woke in an upstairs drawing-room.
The curtains had been pulled back, but the house
was empty. It was furnished and oddly
quiet. A patriarch's monument.
I could see others like it in a kind of park.
Someone had built them long before in a crazed
Scottish-baronial style, foolish with turrets.
Snow had fallen during the night, so I woke
to a white silence. You had gone away.

Was this the estate of some dead, linen
millionaire? And was I some servile spirit
who knew his place in the big house and was locked
in a fierce doctrine of justification?
Somewhere among the firs and beeches, there was
a god of curses who wished us both dead.
His finger was on the trigger. He was insane.
The vindictive shadow, I thought, he scatters
bodies everywhere and has broken the city.

I blamed him then, for I too had been touched;
my notion of freedom was like the curved chairs
in that room. A type of formal elegance.
Had you been there we would have made love
in that strange museum, but it would still
have oppressed us with its fixed anger.
I knew then, in that chill morning, that this
was the house I had lived in once, that I was through
with the polite dust of bibles, the righteous pulpits.

So, later, I woke in a tennis suburb.
History could happen elsewhere, I was free now
in a neat tame place whose gods were milder.
A cold dawn, but a different season.
There was the rickety fizz of starlings
trying to sing, and a grey tenderness.
I was happy then, knowing the days had changed
and that you would come back here, to this room.
You were the season, beyond winter, the first freshness.

What is Fixed to Happen

We know it well, that territory.
It tastes of grit and burning diesel.
A banal sickness as the wheels turn.

The eye is such a cunning despot
We believe its wordless travelogues
And call them *History* or *Let It Happen*.

In those waterfalls of images
Each life is just a simple function
With blank features and one useful skill.

The rain glistens on thick monuments
To an age of lead. That state will fail
Because it must. Pulped bodies happen

In a charred street, and what we know
Is secular : imprisoned shadows
And black plastic shrouds. A public death.

In a scorched space, a broken nowhere,
A homeless grief beyond all grievance
Must suffer nature and be free.

It knows true pity is a rarer love
That asks for neither action nor revenge.
It wills nothing and serves nothing.

Where Art is a Midwife

In the third decade of March,
A Tuesday in the town of Z—

The censors are on day-release.
They must learn about literature.

There are things called ironies,
Also symbols, which carry meaning.

The types of ambiguity
Are as numerous as the enemies

Of the state. Formal and bourgeois,
Sonnets sing of the old order,

Its lost gardens where white ladies
Are served wine in the subtle shade.

This poem about a bear
Is not a poem about a bear.

It might be termed a satire
On a loyal friend. Do I need

To spell it out? Is it possible
That none of you can understand?

Song

A shy innocence is one
Of the customs of my people.

Love in a formal costume
Is a sweet taste on the tongue.

Why, after a year of trouble,
Must the blood flow from my womb?

The Impossible Pictures

In this parable of vengeance
There is a grey newsreel
Being shown inside my head.

What happens is that Lenin's brother
(Aleksandr Ulyanov)
Is being led to execution.

He carries a small book
Wrapped in a piece of cloth.
Is it the Bible or a text

His brother will be forced to write?
He twists it in his hands.
I think he is frightened.

I am wrong, because suddenly
He strikes an officer on the face—
His gestures now are a jerking

Clockwork anachronism.
He is goosestepped to the scaffold.
The frozen yard of the prison

Is like this dawn of rain showers
And heavy lorries, a gull mewling
In its dream of the Atlantic.

Ah, I say, this is Ireland
And my own place, myself.
I see a Georgian rectory

D

Square in the salt winds
Above a broken coast,
And the sea-birds scattering

Their chill cries : I know
That every revenge is nature,
Always on time, like the waves.

Pings on the Great Globe

A baggy gagman and a rubber duck,
Some bits of eggshell on a dirty plate,
The oilcloth with its scurf of crumbs,
Spilt salt, dried yolk and greasy butter.
A litter of newsprint and a stale joke.

Like the snarl of hair burning, its bony pong,
There is a baldness that is brittle.
Unclean! Unclean! The groan of drains,
Their whoop and gritty slabber. Down with
What is done, they glump and splat.

Only the wisest bishop can sit down
To breakfast and call this lovely.
The world is the church of everything
Though an ignorant purity must squat
Among moss and tea leaves in the dank yard.

The Garden of Self-Delight

In that garden to the south
the civil gods are ranged
like statues in a maze
of vines and bay leaves.

The fountain grows a dance
of dreaming surfaces—
none of my slow guesses
will tell how deep they are.

And the men who walk the paths
murmur and hold hands
for they are special friends
who like a fragrant verse.

The taut women pass them by,
virgins of the moon
drifting through the cool
evening in their gowns.

This is a playful place,
though I view it from a bruised
shore that is dark blue
and cold and rigorous.

How can I understand
these fine and gracious beings
who pass me by and sing
lightly to each other?

Saying art is for itself
and prays to mirrors in the sand,
its own mirrors of burnt sand
where the smooth forms look pure.

So tell me there's no law,
and all of life is like a wine
that settles and grows ripe
till it dances on the tongue.

The Other Voice

Anglican firelight.
Jugged hare in a stone house.
The gowned schoolmaster

Has a saintly politeness.
'It is possible to wonder,'
I hear him say.

The wind soughs in the demesne.
Exiles light a candle
To the gods of place.

In the winter darkness
Of this mild village
There is the mossy fragrance

Of damp branches under leaves,
The sour yeast of fungus.
At the lighted doorway

I forget to shake hands.
'We must meet again,' he calls,
And I pretend to pretend.

*

I make that crossing again
And catch the salt freshness
Of early light on Queen's Island.

I lay claim to those marshes,
The Lagan, the shipyards,
The Ormeau Road in winter.

That back room off Donegall Pass,
Remember, where the cell met?
That cupboard of books, tracts and poems?

Plekhanov flares like a firework,
Trotsky crosses Siberia
Turning the pages of Homer,

Raskolnikov wears a long coat
And the end justifies the means.
'Soon the rosewood *meubles*

Will shake in the drawing-rooms
On the Malone Road.
After the long marches

There will be shares for us all
In the means of production.
Songs of a new society

Will grow like flowers
From the barrel of a gun.
It's easy. It's easy.

Love is all you need.'
The record sticks and the party
Spins on forever.

*

We wished it could happen.
Less often now, I wish it still.
For it seems like a barren

Simplicity with no ghosts.
And those dreams of gardens
Called me from the way, saying:

'Here are the small mercies,
A glass of wine, the pungent shade,
And a cagey friendship.

Grace is a volume of Horace,
Bishops and pigeons
Cooing in a woggles shire.

Life, my dear, is a fixed order
And your verse should flow
With a touching sweetness.

Better a civil twilight
Than the level emptiness
Of pulp culture.'

*

In the visions of the night
When deep sleep falls on men,
The flickering pictures

Pass before our eyes.
The fear of necessity
In an absolute narrative.

History is happening:
Tanks and caterpillars,
A moth lying in the dust.

'Once, in Odessa, I watched
The governor cursing.
His back was turned in the hot square.

A regiment with bark sandals,
A sprig of green in their caps.
Their tragedy scorched my mind.

44

Those bark sandals, those green sprigs !
But the process of history
Must scorn an emotion.

I am history now.
I carry time in my mind.
As sharp as an axe.'

*

The actors shake their fists.
I hear the same opinions
In a muddy light.

I see a regiment of clones
Waving their arms and shouting :
A glossy brutalism dances

To a parody of song.
Identikit opinions
In the camps of the punks.

The theatre is in the streets,
The streets are in the theatre,
The poet is torn to pieces.

*

What does a poem serve?
Only the pure circle of itself.
Now, between two coasts,

The servants of the state
Doze to the drum of engines.
Hammered stars, a dark dream,

The hard night in a dead bowl.
Where a free light wakes
To its spacious language

Choice is still possible.
I dream of a subtle voice,
Stare in a mirror and pray

To a shadow wandering
Beyond the cold shores
And tides of the Baltic.

                    *

In Buddhist Moscow,
In lamp-eyed St. Petersburg,
Mandelstam is walking

Through the terrible night.
His lips are moving
In a lyric ripple.

The syllables chirp
Like a dolphin, lost
In the grey depths of the state.

'As I walk through the dark
I will tell you this:
That morning, in the buttery

Of the Kremlin, I left
Because I could never stay
In the same room as Trotsky.

Do you understand me?
Those ideals will fit you
Like a feral uniform.

Hear how the wolves howl,
Functions of nature
On the frozen plains.

All the dry glitters
In your cento of memories
Will never catch

The living truth on the wing.
The bird has flown its nest
And the snow weighs

On the gothic branches,
Lavish and cruel, like power.
What cadences, what rich voices

Have you hardened against?
What images have you broken?
In the great dome of art

(It was this we longed for
In our Petropolis)
I am free of history.

Beyond dust and rhetoric,
In the meadows of the spirit
I kiss the Word.'

Cross on a Circle

The island funeral
Is an open boat
Between coasts,
Men with Aran faces
And shawled women
By the metric coffin,
Its hard angles
On a celtic sea.

Every day I cross
A glistening stretch
Of inland water
And for one moment
The light shrills,
Faithful, travelling
Towards a ghost's
Yeasty tomorrow,
Or yesterday, is it,
In the damp acres?

Man with Hookah

The hot afternoon is all middle.
A white balcony shrills,
A pile of green fodder is the same green,
And the oxen are beaten by the sun.
The man squatting on a straw mat
Has made his body gleam with mustard oil
And like a wrestler or illusionist
He will escape from this locked vision
When smoke is coaxed, in bubbles, through the scented water
In a clay vase.
Already he is sliding out
Of the hard day, its glaring surface.
The crowd in the bazaar
Feels the warm dust between its toes.
Only a woman in a lime-green sari
Walks on water where she goes.
The glans of a cobra
Preens itself, and the air trembles
In its chains.

The light turns milky and a fine gauze
Settles on the fields
Where men in white pyjamas
Move
Not going anywhere but where they are.
Three musicians play an evening *rag* :
The music circles on itself,
A brittle glistening
That never breaks.
That cow, that bus, that mound of dung,
The spirit touches everything.
His lips are subtle on the mouthpiece now.
One yoni and one lingam,

One dream inside another.
Ecstasy is a lake
That grows the lotus,
And those smiling couples with their long noses
And oval eyes
Swim playfully inside a graceful love.

A Lyric Afterwards

There was a taut dryness all that summer
and you sat each day in the hot garden
until those uniformed comedians
filled the street with their big white ambulance,
fetching you and bringing you back to me.

Far from the sea of ourselves we waited
and prayed for the tight blue silence to give.
In your absence I climbed to a square room
where there were dried flowers, folders of sonnets
and crossword puzzles : call them musical

snuffboxes or mannered anachronisms,
they were all too uselessly intricate,
caskets of the dead spirit. Their bitter
constraints and formal pleasures were a style
of being perfect in despair; they spoke

with the vicious trapped crying of a wren.
But that is changed now, and when I see you
walking by the river, a step from me,
there is this great kindness everywhere :
now in the grace of the world and always.